IDEAS Plus

A Collection of Practical Teaching Ideas

Book Nine

National Council of Teachers of English
1111 Kenyon Road, Urbana, Illinois 61801

Staff Editors: Jane M. Curran, Michelle Sanden Johlas

Cover Design: Carlton Bruett; Illustrations: Richard Maul

Interior Book Design: Tom Kovacs for TGK Design

NCTE Stock Number: 22663

Library of Congress Catalog Card Number 84-3479

IDEAS Plus is published in August by the National Council of Teachers of English as an exclusive benefit of *NCTE Plus* membership. *NCTE Plus* membership also includes four issues of *NOTES Plus* (ISSN 0738-86-24), published in October, December, January, and March. Annual membership dues are $55.00; $15.00 of this amount is for *NOTES Plus* and *IDEAS Plus*. Inquiries about *NCTE Plus* membership or communications regarding change of address and permission to reprint should be addressed to *NOTES Plus*, 1111 Kenyon Road, Urbana, IL 61801. *POSTMASTER:* Send address changes to *NOTES Plus*, 1111 Kenyon Road, Urbana, IL 61801. Second-class postage paid at Champaign, Illinois, and at additional mailing offices.

Contents

Foreword

IDEAS Plus and its quarterly companion *NOTES Plus* are the principal benefits of *NCTE Plus* membership. *IDEAS Plus* is sent out at the end of the summer so that teachers will have it in hand as they begin the school year.

The ideas collected in this ninth edition of *IDEAS Plus* come from two sources: ideas submitted at an Idea Exchange session at an NCTE Annual Convention or Spring Conference, and contributions by readers of *NOTES Plus* and *IDEAS Plus*.

1 Language Exploration

Language is the vital ingredient for conveying our thoughts clearly and concisely. The activities in this section will stimulate critical thinking and will encourage students to express these thoughts in creative, imaginative ways. Through the teaching strategies gathered here, students become acquainted with another student, express themselves through a personalized license plate, take a stand on a controversial issue, find an outlet for expressing criticism, and post their views on books and reading. Included are across the curriculum activities that highlight the role of language and ideas that feature figurative language, concrete descriptions of abstract terms, and taking possession of favorite words.

Making Introductions

I use the following interview activity at the beginning of the year, when students are new to me and to one another. It is a long procedure, taking five to seven class periods, and may easily be adapted or personalized by other teachers.

Step 1. Students begin by creating twenty to twenty-five questions that they would ask someone if they wanted to learn more about that person. I might model types of questions used by interviewers, explaining that everyone conducts a type of interview when introduced to someone new. Two students might role-play an interview as if they were meeting for the first time. This activity takes about half of a class period.

Step 2. Students discuss the questions on their lists. We look for ways to group the kinds of questions, usually coming up with the following categories:

personal information—height, weight, hair color, eye color, age, birthdate

family information—size of family, number of siblings, placement within family, parents' occupations hobbies and activities—hobbies, sports played, church activities, civic activities, school clubs and groups, jobs, special interests

personal interests—favorites in music, food, colors, movies, books, clothes, TV shows

goals—immediate and long-term

I usually suggest that students each come up with about five questions per category, but the number of questions in each category is up to them. As a homework assignment, students restructure, rewrite, and categorize their questions.

Step 3. Each student pairs up with one other student. Any random method of grouping is recommended. If the pairing leaves an extra student, that student may interview the teacher or may be assigned to work with a pair of students. Students ask their partner the questions they have devised, monitoring and adjusting questions as necessary. Students may refrain from answering any questions that they feel are too personal or too embarrassing, but usually students are eager to respond. The interviewer records all responses. Then students switch roles, and the interviewed students begin asking questions. I monitor students carefully to ensure that they are interviewing one another.

Step 4. When the questioning is completed, students work individually to create an essay describing their particular partner. The grouping of questions into categories will lead into essay writing. I usually ask students to evaluate their partner's essay and to suggest revisions. Rough drafts, including questions and responses, are turned in with the final drafts. I grade the papers mainly on organizational skills. This step takes one to two class periods.

Step 5. I model a speech introducing myself (or the unpaired student in the class); then we discuss appropriate speech-making techniques. After a short rehearsal with their partners, students introduce their partners to the entire class. Students often read their essays aloud, but I encourage them to include anecdotes that may not appear in the essay. Peer evaluation of the presentations may determine part of the grade. The time spent on the presentations is based on the number of students in the class. A maximum time limit could be imposed on the speeches.

Gail P. Hacker, North Charleston High School, North Charleston, South Carolina

Personalized Plates

Like many other teachers, I begin each year with an activity that introduces students to me and to their classmates. By the end of the activity, we know each other better, and I have an interesting, colorful bulletin board.

I begin the activity by writing on the chalkboard examples of personalized license plates using letters and numbers. Plates might identify a sport, a hobby, or a special interest (such as PLAY BALL or HACKER) or might be descriptive (such as BLUE EYES). Students talk about what each example reveals about its owner and are encouraged to suggest other examples.

After the discussion, each student prepares a list of objects or descriptive terms that give clues to his or her identity. Students then use their lists to create their own personalized license plates. I have students use up to seven letters, numbers, and spaces since this is the format for most states, but some students might find this restrictive.

I hand out sheets of paper containing a rectangle in which students stencil their license plate letters and numbers and several lines on which they explain why the plate is appropriate.

Here is an example of one student's license plate and explanation:

> S.T.O.P.
> Students teaching other peers (S.T.O.P.) is an organization which I helped to begin. It involves students sharing their knowledge with other students about drugs and alcohol. Many fun activities were planned to teach younger children about the dangers of alcohol and drugs, including cigarettes. I would very much like to see S.T.O.P. being started in other schools. I think it would help teach many of my peers how to stop before they start.
>
> Victoria F.

After students complete their license plates, they might create bumper stickers that deliver a special message, either related to their license plates or indicating other aspects of their identity. We display both the license plates and the bumper stickers on a bulletin board captioned "They'll drive you crazy."

Sandra K. Mullally, Walter D. Johnson Junior High School, Las Vegas, Nevada

Four Corners

I discovered this idea while reading Jenny Davis's second young adult novel, *Sex Education* (Dell, 1989). Characters in this novel participate in a fun, motivational classroom activity called Four Corners. Designed to promote lively discussion, Four Corners encourages students to take a stand—literally—on important issues.

Here's how it works. The teacher reads aloud a thought-provoking, often controversial, statement. Students decide if they (1) strongly agree, (2) agree, (3) disagree, or (4) strongly disagree with the statement; then they move to the corresponding corner of the room. After a brief discussion within the group, each group presents its arguments in an attempt to win members from the opposing corners. Once the four groups have presented their platforms, students reevaluate their initial choice and take a final stand, either by staying where they are or by moving to another corner.

I have expanded Davis's idea to integrate journal writing. Students first sort through their feelings on the issue by freewriting in journals. Then they move to a corner of the room, acting more on their written reflections than on peer pressure. After the four corners present their arguments, students return to their desks, freewrite about the views that they have heard, and formulate their decisions before making their final stands known. In addition, students might write a commentary about the final outcome, responding to such questions as, How do you account for these results? Is the final outcome what you expected? Why or why not? What did you learn about the subject that you didn't know before?

This versatile activity could be incorporated across the disciplines and throughout most grade levels. Students would be writing to learn about issues, themselves, and their classmates, and, consequently, about how each affects the others. No passive one-way learning here! Four Corners will get your students thinking, moving, and writing.

Diane Tomczak, Delta College, University Center, Michigan

Complaint Department

One February our school was closed for two days due to snow. When we returned to school, the principal announced that the two days would be made up on a Saturday during April and an additional day added at the end of the school year. My eighth graders were enraged. Their euphoria over the unexpected two-day holiday was immediately replaced by anger over the makeup days. At that moment I decided that the lesson listed in my plan book was far less important than a lesson in constructive expression of feelings.

I began by guiding a discussion about placing blame where blame is due. Students quickly realized that the principal did not mandate the Indiana laws that all schools in our state have to follow. We moved on to look at the reasoning behind several new public education laws, such as a longer school year and strict limitations in class size at the primary level. Then we discussed several ways to express ourselves in order to produce results.

The tone of the classroom had relaxed considerably by the time we shared humorous stories about the tactics of getting our own way. I asked students, "How do you convince your mom to buy that new pair of jeans that you want? Do you scream and yell, or do you try a more diplomatic approach?" Students agreed that perhaps diplomacy had proven useful a time or two.

Before ending our discussion, I felt obligated to comment on the responsibilities that accompany any criticism. I explained that as a critic, you must anticipate as accurately as possible the response of your audience. You must weigh the consequences of your actions.

In this case we felt we could speak our minds freely without serious repercussions. But I asked students to consider situations where they might not voice their complaints so freely. Nikki brought up criticizing an employer. "You would have to decide if what you had to say was worth risking your job over." Raina added, "What if you had kids to feed?"

This discussion opened the door for a writing assignment. I asked students to write a letter to the governor, using their newfound diplomatic skills. They were to explain their complaint about the makeup school days, back it up with evidence, and propose a solution. This letter did not have to be mailed, but students had the option of doing so if they wished. I agreed to help polish content and format; alternately, peer-editing partners or groups could help with this task. The final versions were well-planned, courteous letters that even the opposition would be proud of.

Students are thinking, feeling individuals whose opinions are deserving of consideration. All they generally seem to lack are the social skills and experience of emotional expression. It is my feeling that bolstering their basic communication skills encourages responsible expression in our often highly emotional students.

Roberta A. Gutwein, Linton-Stockton Junior High School, Linton, Indiana

Language Arts Week

Our high school underscores the importance of language in everyday life by designating "Language Arts Week" once each year. Different activities are featured each day, and the week ends with a booth displaying the language-related projects at the weekend basketball game.

Each day of Language Arts Week the Pledge of Allegiance is said in both English and another language. We choose languages taught in the school so that students can join in or pick out familiar words. We also ask exchange students or other students from different countries to recite the pledge in their native languages. English-speaking students enjoy hearing the various versions of the pledge.

One day of Language Arts Week is designated as Character Day. Students and teachers each select a favorite literary character, usually one from a work read in class, and then come to school dressed as that character. Students are encouraged to act the part of their characters, which usually means placing these characters in different settings and circumstances from the novels or stories that we read. Students attempt to identify their classmates, and a prize might go to the student who correctly names the most characters. To encourage participation, teachers might award extra-credit points to those students who take on the role of literary characters. At least a portion of the English class that day might be devoted to a conversation between different characters.

Another day is T-shirt/Sweatshirt Day. Students and teachers design language shirts on any topic from literature to grammar to writing. Students might depict or create with words a setting from a work of literature, or they might reproduce a quotation from a favorite literary character. Other students might choose a line of poetry or might even write their own limericks. The shirt designing could be a classtime project or could be done out of school. We have a schoolwide contest to name the most original shirt.

A favorite day at our school is Extra-Credit Day. Students may turn in any creative project that is related to a topic studied in their English classes. These projects have included posters, bookcovers, drawings, dioramas, needlework, ceramics, woodwork, papier-mâché, masks, maps, and more. In addition to demonstrating students' artistic talents, the projects help connect language to visual elements. These extra-credit projects are displayed within the classroom during the week and then gathered for exhibit at the basketball game.

Throughout the week, literary techniques are used in an unusual way. Morning announcements include at least one example of figurative language. Similes, metaphors, personification, limericks, onomatopoeia, and antithesis add a new dimension to announcements about club meetings, lunch-hour schedules, and intramural scores. Teachers enjoy writing these announcements, and students make a list of all the figures of speech that they can identify. To promote attention, we give an award to the student who "catches" the most examples of figurative language. A related project might have students write their own examples of figurative language.

The last day of the week introduces another genre into the language arts curriculum. We have used Billy Joel's song "We Didn't Start the Fire" as inspiration for a writing project. Students compile lists of events in their own lives, thereby adding to the lyrics of the song. We show a taped interview of Billy Joel explaining how he viewed the creative process. Students follow his example to add their own verses to his song.

By the end of the week, students have seen firsthand the important role that language plays in our lives.

Debbie Bushart, Marshall County High School, Benton, Kentucky

I Own That Word!

The first time I say, "Oh, I just love that word—I love the way it feels as it trips across my lips," the students in my eleventh-grade English class simultaneously roll their eyes, smirk, and look at me as if they think, "Boy, this teacher's really nuts."

I agree with Robert L. Hillerich, who contends in *Teaching Children to Write, K–8* (Prentice Hall, 1985) that "the best single way to develop vocabulary—receptive or expressive, and in adult or child—is through enjoyable exposure to words in a variety of contexts, with an interest in language" (p. 83). I love words and want to share this love with my students. I want to help them develop a similar feeling for words.

Since the love of words cannot be taught in a structured lesson, I demonstrate my love spontaneously throughout the school year. Whenever I say or read a word that I especially like, I talk about that word with my class. I also share some of my favorite words with them, words like *vicarious* and *bibliophile*. I do not talk about the definition of the word at this time. Instead, I talk about how wonderful the word feels and sounds as it trips across my lips.

It does not take students long to realize that I am serious about my love of words. They begin to share words that they find interesting. This leads to a relaxed and playful attitude toward the learning of new words. Hillerich suggests that the teacher should "call attention to that unusual word, that perfectly chosen word, that melodious word, or that new word" (p. 101). I believe that if the teacher can get students hooked on words, the students' vocabulary will grow.

Our sharing of interesting words leads us into a discussion of ownership of words and the importance of using words that we own in our writing. I explain to students that to have ownership of a word, they must know the meaning of the word, know how to use the word correctly, feel comfortable using the word, and feel that the word belongs to them. This keeps them from selecting words in the thesaurus and using them haphazardly and incorrectly.

Often during the year I tell my students that I own a particular word, but that I will loan it to them. They in turn come to class with new words to use and to share with me. One group of girls would come to class each day with a new word that they claimed they owned. We had fun playing with the words, and they acquired numerous new words. The following year I overheard one student in her English class across the hall still claiming, "I own that word!"

Pat DeFloria, the head of our English department, transferred the idea of ownership of words into a vocabulary activity. Students divided into groups of three or four. For this activity she let them choose the members of their particular group. Each group selected four interesting, unusual words from different chapters of *Lord of the Flies*, the novel that they were currently reading. Using visual aids, students were to "sell" these words to the class in some creative way. Some students did TV commercials; some used the *Sesame Street* format. One girl dressed in a raincoat and, as a word pusher, furtively opened her coat, revealing the words she had to sell. One boy arrived as Word Man with a cardboard WM emblem on his shirt. Interestingly, some of these words appeared in writing that the students later did.

Teaching vocabulary through vocabulary books and lists of vocabulary words encountered while reading does not work. This idea was reinforced during a summer writing institute I attended in Texas, based on the New Jersey Writing Project, which advocates incorporating spelling and grammar into the writing process. It supports my idea that written vocabulary can be expanded by everyday usage and a feeling for words.

Beverly L. Greeney, Eisenhower High School, Houston, Texas

Great Questions

I use the following activity to get students thinking about some major questions about science.

I start by passing out a list of "The 20 Greatest Unanswered Questions of Science" that appeared in *Science Digest* (1985, vol. 93, no. 10, pp. 34–61, continued). The questions deal with some of the major mysteries of the universe, such as

How did life begin?

What happened to the dinosaurs?

Will we ever control the weather?

How does a cell become a complex creature?

Other questions pertain to photosynthesis, evolution, supercomputers, and eternity.

Students are to read through this article and select a topic to investigate. If they wish, they may propose their own important question. And if they discover a new topic of interest during their investigation, they may switch topics once they get an approval from me.

We spend several days in the library as students locate information on their particular topic. The information might include current essays on the topic, articles in scientific magazines, and newspaper accounts of recent experiments or discoveries. I recommend that students make use of the following sources of information: the card catalog, the *Reader's Guide to Periodical Literature*, and the staff librarians. I also point out some excellent writings by cross-disciplinary thinkers (writers like Stephen Hawking or Lewis Thomas). If, and only if, printed sources are not available, I might authorize sociological methods instead.

The second part of the assignment is for students to present the information on their topic in an oral report to the class. I emphasize that they are to explain their topic, what information they found, and how they felt about what they found. The topics are complex, so some of the information they uncover may be difficult to understand. Students will need to explain this information in terms that their classmates will understand. When several people are researching the same topic, I allow group reports as long as the reporting responsibilities are shared. I suggest a time length of five to ten minutes, but I let students know that their talks may run longer if they notify me at the time I schedule the reports. For those nervous about oral presentations, I explain, "You may read from notes as long as you glance up at the audience at least five times."

We talk about presenting information orally so that students understand what I feel is important: effective voice projection, a clear and logical presentation, and being informative.

Carl R. Steiner, Ferndale High School, Ferndale, Washington

Angling In on Alliteration

While discussing alliteration with my tenth graders, I had a sudden inspiration for an activity that might bring them deeper understanding of the term. As a brief homework assignment, each student was to write an alliterative sentence using his or her name as the subject. Here are some of their efforts:

> Vivacious Veronica vetoed the victorious vote.

Mean Michele moved madly through the mall on Monday after meeting Mimi at Maurice's and purchasing many multicolored, maroon, and mauve mittens for Mom.

Shonda sat on a stack of stickpins and got sick to her stomach.

Latreece likes to lick big luscious lollipops while listening to the latest lyrics on the radio.

Tonya told Tammy on the telephone that Todd had taken Tiffany to Taco Bell.

Reading the sentences aloud the following day demonstrated my students' creativity and provided some interesting fun with tongue twisters. The exercise took little time, provided a break from more serious discussion, and helped students remember what alliteration is.

Holly M. Westcott, Wilson High School, Florence, South Carolina

Replace Graffiti with Across the Curriculum Writing

This year, inspired student writing transformed the hallways of our middle school. Student papers and photographs replaced the graffiti, and students eagerly lined up to read what their classmates had written. With across the curriculum involvement, the walls of your school can also come alive. Interested? Here's how it was done in my school.

The principal started the activity by requesting that all teachers submit the best examples of student writing on a content-related topic. It was up to the teachers to select the topic for the writing assignment. One of our math teachers, María Muñoz, challenged her students to describe themselves in mathematical terminology, prompting a student to begin her essay, "At school, I am the part of the number in front of the decimal."

In your school, student writings might focus on a particular theme, such as an autobiographical essay, with the particular content matter shaped by the different class subjects. Journal entries, short stories, and poetry are all appropriate. The project might run many weeks to allow one individual class to display writing samples each week, or several classes could be featured at a time. Since all classes at our school participated, students of all ability levels were published on the walls.

Once the writing was completed, each teacher selected the best writing samples within the class. Students might discuss what standards should be used in determining the best examples of the assignment and might help make the final selections. These writings and an accompanying photograph were slated for display in the trophy case, but writings and photos of all students could be posted outside each classroom. The name of the class whose work was on display could be announced each week on the public-address system.

Students paused between classes to read the writing samples and to talk about writing rather than scribble on the walls, gossip, or fight. This refreshing student behavior gives validity to Kirby and Liner's contention that "a display of finished products . . . stimulates talk and thinking about writing" (*Inside Out: Developmental Strategies for Teaching Writing*, Boynton and Cook, 1981, p. 217).

Maybe across the curriculum publishing will melt some of the graffiti from your school walls, as it did in ours.

Lurlene Grayer Adams, Rogers Middle School, San Antonio, Texas

The Power of Observation

I use a subtle activity to teach my high school students a little lesson in the power of observation.

Without the rest of the class knowing, I select one student in advance to take careful notes of everything that occurs during one class period. I caution the student to pay heed to dialogue, material taught, students' questions, and events that occur during class.

I might arrange for a phone call (we have phones in our classrooms) or a brief interruption from a colleague or a student from another class. I also make certain there is a sustained dialogue with one or two students. The rest of the class is conducted as usual.

The following day I ask students to write down everything that they remember occurring in class on the previous day. That's my sole direction. I allow about ten to fifteen minutes.

We then discuss the "day after" remembrance compared to the "on the spot" dialogue recorded by my secret scribe. While at least one student will indicate that "nothing" happened the previous day, the other papers will vary greatly in the amount of information reported, as well as in the words chosen to describe events. There might also be a difference in the way a single event is recorded. Those students who were involved in the sustained discussion with me will write a first-person account, while others in the class who merely observed the interchange will take on the voice of a third person. Thus students learn firsthand about the importance of voice in writing narratives.

This is a simple activity, but it allows students to experience and participate in a focused exercise concerning observation, perception, and description of events.

Lynn P. Dieter, Maine East High School, Park Ridge, Illinois

Introducing Figurative Language

I introduce my middle school students to figurative language through the use of quotations from famous people employing different examples of figurative language. Here are a few of the quotations I distribute:

1. Character is like a tree and reputation like its shadow. The shadow is what we think of it; the tree is the real thing. (Abraham Lincoln)
2. We cannot expect that all nations will adopt like systems, for conformity is the jailer of freedom and the enemy of growth. (John F. Kennedy)
3. Courage is fear that has said its prayers. (Karle Baker)
4. When one door of happiness closes, another opens; but often we look so long at the closed door that we do not see the one which has been opened for us. (Helen Keller)
5. If a man does not keep pace with his companions, perhaps it is because he hears a different drummer. Let him step to the music he hears, however measured or far away. (Henry David Thoreau)

I took these examples from *The World Book Complete Word Power Library* (World Book-Child Craft, 1981). Other books containing quotations would also be good sources of figurative language.

We go through the quotations one by one, discussing what each means and how the speaker's meaning is affected by the choice of language. We determine both the literal level and the figurative level of the examples and examine how the choice of words helps the speakers clarify their meanings and make their words memorable.

Next we look more closely at the various types of figurative language. Without providing definitions, I give one or two examples of each type and encourage students to come up with their own definitions. If they have trouble, I prompt them by asking what characteristics the examples have in common. Here are some of the sample sentences I use:

Simile
His nose is as red as a cherry because of his cold.
The boy ran like a scared rabbit.

Metaphor
The stars are diamonds twinkling in the night sky.
My daughter is the light of my life.

Personification
The siren screamed through the quiet city.
Death was knocking at his door.

Metonymy
The dish that you cooked for dinner was delicious.
My shoes hurt.

Synecdoche
Keep an eye on this.
Give me a hand.

Hyperbole
I am so hungry I could eat a horse.
I've got a ton of homework.

Understatement
After breaking all of Mother's china, I was in a little trouble.
After running ten miles, I was a little out of breath.

Irony
Although they had won the television, the poor family had no electricity.
The fat man's name was "Slim."

To complete our examination of figurative language, I borrow an idea from Carole B. Bencich in *Activities to Promote Critical Thinking* (ed. Jeff Golub, NCTE, 1986, pp. 7–10). Students write a metaphor that describes some aspect of their own personalities. Then they create a poster, using original artwork or pictures cut from magazines, that gives a visual representation of the metaphor. Statements like "I am a paper clip, determined to hold things together" or "I am a piano keyboard; I can send out a beautiful melody or a harsh mixture of sounds, depending on my mood" easily lend themselves to depiction. The resulting posters are displayed for all to read and enjoy.

Elizabeth C. Brooks, Simmons Middle School, Birmingham, Alabama

Bulletin Board Beliefs

Since students usually listen to other students far more readily than to teachers, give them a chance to express themselves about their reading. Here are the steps I follow.

1. Cover the bulletin board with colorful papers or burlap.
2. Buy or construct a decorative border for the board.
3. Label the board "The Truth, the Whole Truth, and Nothing But the Truth" or a similar caption. Students might try naming the board themselves.
4. Attach to the board as many book-related objects as you can locate: book jackets, cartoons, short magazine articles, letters to the editor, editorials, brief short stories, word puzzles, illustrations of authors. Rotate these periodically.
5. Keep a pile of 3″ × 5″ index cards near the bulletin board. Encourage students to respond in writing to any topic related to books or to opinions already posted and to add their cards in collage fashion to the board.

The board might seem a little barren at first, but soon students will be eager to post their opinions and to read what their classmates have to say in response.

Raphael Johstoneaux, Jr., Brigham Young University, Provo, Utah

Defining the Abstract

I use the following activity to help my students understand how the concrete defines the abstract. The exercise is a good introduction to writing a description of a character or a place, to studying poetry, or simply to understanding the connotation of words.

We start with a brief discussion of abstract terms and the difficulty in defining them. Then I give students a handout on which appear the following words:

color
smell
taste
sound
texture
shape
object
animal
food
beverage
clothing
place
flower
weather
country
building
car
music
game
movie star

My list is chosen to evoke specific, concrete images. Other teachers might choose to add or subtract categories.

I explain that the assignment is to select an abstract word (such as *joy, sorrow, wisdom,* or *cleverness*) and then to fill in the concrete image evoked by the abstract term under each category on the list. We work through an example together so that students understand that they must be specific. Our class list might resemble the following example for the abstract term *joy:*

color: royal blue
smell: fresh bread baking
taste: sweet, rich
sound: waterfall
texture: highly polished wood
shape: round
object: brightly wrapped present
animal: purring cat
food: chocolate chip cookie
beverage: cherry soda
clothing: lacy party dress
place: Disney World
flower: yellow daffodils
weather: sunny, warm
country: Switzerland
building: roller rink
car: red Corvette convertible
music: Madonna
game: Old Maid
movie star: Tony Danza

Then students select their own abstract nouns. I ask them to think for a while before they begin their lists. They should be sure that what they write clearly reflects their feelings of the abstract word. I also remind them to be specific—to write "red hatchback Pinto" rather than simply "Ford."

When the lists are completed, they can be shared with a partner or with the class as a whole. Students who picked the same abstract term might compare lists and see how differently they view the same concept.

Carol J. Bakle, Snider High School, Fort Wayne, Indiana

Learning Irony through Humor

In my experience with remedial-level college students, I have learned that they often have difficulty identifying and discussing irony and related figures of speech in the literature they read. Though I do not in general use literary elements as a way into short stories, I often find it useful to take a break from journals and personal responses to look at the topic of irony for a few days.

About two weeks before beginning this mini-unit, I ask students to notice, in their conversations with classmates and others, instances of people saying the opposite of what they mean or speaking in an exaggerated or understated manner; for example, "That was really smart" (when a friend nearly steps in front of a car), "I almost died" (from embarrassment), or "I guess the movie was sort of funny" (when all present had been laughing hysterically). Students write these quotations down, and at each subsequent class meeting I ask them to report on what they are hearing, so that I am confident they know what to listen for, and so that they receive frequent reminders. The data that they collect over the two-week interval forms the basis of our discussion of verbal irony: understatement, overstatement or hyperbole, and saying the opposite of what is meant. We go over the differences between these different figures of speech, with students providing examples of each from their notes.

Next, I use cartoons to demonstrate the use of irony to students. Working in groups of four, students examine two sets of cartoons and decide what makes them funny. The cartoons in each set share a single underlying principle. In one group it is the situation itself that is funny—such as a cow using a straw to drink milk from a glass. In the second group the humor comes because the viewer can see (or knows) something unknown to the cartoon characters—such as a joke based on the earth being flat. Through examination and discussion of the cartoons, students discover the concepts of situational and dramatic irony.

After defining for ourselves the concepts of dramatic, situational, and verbal irony, we turn to three very short stories: "The Chaser" by John Collier (dramatic irony), "The Cop and the Anthem" by O. Henry (situational irony), and "Why I Live at the P.O." by Eudora Welty (verbal irony). Students work in groups, reading each story and deciding what type of irony is present. We then discuss all the stories as a class, and students complete the unit by writing a brief paper defining and illustrating one type of irony.

Elise Ann Earthman, San Francisco State University, California

Quick Communication

Sometimes our middle school students need a change-of-pace activity. This fun procedure will have your students begging for more time to write.

Students will need at least ten sheets of plain paper, cut in note-size squares. Select two or three students to be runners.

When the activity begins, no one is to speak aloud. Instead, students pass notes back and forth to each other. Each note is to be folded once, with "To" and "From" on the outside. (We find that the "From" line discourages inappropriate comments.) Then the student holds the note in the air, and a runner picks it up and delivers it.

After a few minutes notes will begin moving fast and furiously. We write notes too, especially to those students who may not be receiving notes. Runners can be rotated midway through the activity so that everyone gets a chance to write.

We do not spend a lot of time on this activity, but it is an opportunity to reinforce the importance of language. Establishing some guidelines about the topic of the notes might make this useful as a prewriting activity.

Sherry Royer and Bonnie Kern, Eagleview Middle School, Colorado Springs, Colorado

2 Literature

While we might hope that students would find our delight in literature contagious, we realize that developing an appreciation of literature is not to be taken for granted. The activities that follow will help students become involved with literature and recognize its potential to enrich our lives. Among the strategies are teaming contemporary musicians with Puritan writers, placing mythological characters in present-day settings, and learning through collaboration. In addition, there are ideas for assisting with book selection, familiarizing students with library resources, and providing an alternative to the standard book review.

Selecting the Right Book

Our students are regularly assigned outside reading in books of their choice, but all too often length is the criterion for selection, or just any book is hurriedly checked out as library time runs out. To solve the problem, I enlisted the school librarian's aid in helping students select appropriate books.

Based on the level of ability of students in my classes, the librarian pulls out suitable books in the following general categories: adventure, fantasy, mystery, romance, science fiction, sports, teen problems. The books are grouped in stacks of five books from different categories. If several of my classes are completing the assignment on the same day, the librarian will need to fill in with additional books as books are checked out.

When my students enter the library, they take a stack of books and a Novel Selection Process sheet, which asks students to answer the following questions for each book:

1. The cover is _____ ordinary, _____ interesting, _____ boring.
2. Check the descriptions that apply to the printing in the book:

_____ easy to read
_____ too small
_____ not enough space between lines
_____ margins too narrow

3. Read the *blurb* (the summary on the inside book jacket) and any reviews on the back cover. In one or two sentences tell what the story is about.
4. Read the first page of the novel and explain what you learn from it.
5. What type of novel is it?

_____ adolescence
_____ adventure
_____ fantasy
_____ horror/supernatural
_____ romance
_____ sports
_____ teenage problems
_____ other: __________

6. Rate the book:

_____ I wouldn't read this book, even if it were the only one in the library.
_____ It looks interesting, but not for me.
_____ I might read this book, but not this year.
_____ I would probably like this book.
_____ I am going to read this book.

(Students fill out a form for each of their five books, but to conserve the school paper supply, I ask them to fill out one form and to use their own paper to answer the questions for the remaining books.)

After students complete the information for each book, they each select one book from their stack of five to read for the class assignment.

The procedure helps students to apply criteria other than length and to select books that are potentially of interest to them. Gone are the arguments about whether a student's book is acceptable for a class assignment, yet students exercise some choice in their reading materials.

Cinde S. Bordes, St. Thomas More Catholic High School, Lafayette, Louisiana

Library Search

Teaching students to use basic library resources can all too often involve looking up information that is meaningless and unimportant to them. Since the use of the card catalog and the *Reader's Guide to Periodical Literature* is an essential part of our unit on study skills and library orientation, I devised a method to use students' own interests to assess their understanding of these library resources.

On the first day of class each year, students fill out a general information sheet that includes questions about their interests, hobbies, and books that they have recently read. A few weeks later as part of their library orientation, I use these answers for an individualized exercise in the library. I hand each student a worksheet, personalized with their own interests, like the following:

> Use the card catalog to locate two books on _skiing_.
> Give the following information about each book. Remember that all of this information is on the card in the card catalog.

	Book #1	Book #2
Title	________	________
Author	________	________
Call Number	________	________
Publisher	________	________
Date Published	________	________

> Use the card catalog to locate the following book or a book by the author listed.

	Book #1	Book #2
Title	________	_White Fang_
Author	_Ray Bradbury_	________
Call Number	________	________
Publisher	________	________

> Use the *Reader's Guide to Periodical Literature* to locate two magazine articles about _skateboarding_.

	Article #1	Article #2
Magazine	________	________
Article	________	________
Volume Number	________	________
Date	________	________
Page Numbers	________	________

Now, select one of the magazine articles you located above. Fill out the request form and present it to a librarian at the desk. Read the article and write a brief summary of the article on the back of this paper.

I fill in the blanks with a personal interest, such as football, soccer, backpacking, cheerleading, jazz, computers, fashion, or even telephones for those who indicate they spend their time talking on the phone, and students are to locate two books and two magazine articles on two different topics. I also specify one book by title and one book by a specific author, which students are to locate by using the card catalog.

Although preparing an individual assignment for each student takes extra time, the rewards are many. Students are delighted to use their personal interests for an assignment. They are motivated to use the library resources and require little prodding to complete the assignment. Best of all, once they locate books and magazines that interest them personally, they are more apt to read the material.

Brenda Piccone, Amphitheater High School, Tucson, Arizona

Not Another Book Report, Please!

I'm not sure who dreads book reports more, the teacher or the student. Since our department requires outside reading in all English classes, I wanted to come up with an assignment that would be both meaningful to the students and a pleasure for teachers to read.

I have used the following format for short stories and novels with students in grades 10 through 12. Junior high teachers have used it as well. The beauty of the report form is that it discourages copying or faking, and it lends itself to genuine commentary. The different types of writing elicited by the report form are indicated in parentheses.

Here is the information I request on my Generic Reading Report form:

1. *Full title, author's name, copyright date, and number of pages:* For a novel or play, underline the title; for a short story, use quotation marks.
2. *Give a brief summary of the plot:* Must be no more than seven sentences long. (Report of information)

3. *Explain the significance of the title:* Authors do not choose a title randomly. Usually there is an important reason and the title is symbolic. (Reflection, speculation)
4. *Describe your first impressions of the main character:* Give examples to explain your ideas. (Observation)
5. *Identify what caused a change in the main character and explain how the character changed:* These changes may have been a consequence of choice, a conflict of some kind that has to be resolved, a display of some outstanding trait like courage, or even a result of events that occur during the novel. (Interpretation)
6. *Cite a memorable passage from the book:* Copy word for word a short passage that you thought was worth remembering. Explain why you chose this passage from the book. (Evaluation, possibly autobiographical)
7. *Read all of the following questions and then write one response about the significance of reading this literary work:* What discovery did you make as a result of reading this book? What change occurred in your life after reading this book? Did you receive any enlightenment? Did the book affirm your views on life in some way? In other words, what did you get out of reading this book? (Reflection)

Josephine D. Zarro, Manual Arts High School, Los Angeles, California

Simple Character Analysis

I use the following activity with my ninth-grade students to lead into a simple character analysis. It has worked successfully with characters like Rainsford in Richard Connell's "The Most Dangerous Game" and Luther in Jay Neugeboren's "Luther." The procedure is most effective with characters who undergo great changes, because they generate the most diverse list of adjectives.

After we have read a short story, students work individually to list five adjectives describing the main character. We make a composite list on the chalkboard, with each student contributing one adjective at a time until all the adjectives on their lists are on the board.

Students study the composite list for pairs of antonyms. For "Luther," pairs included *intelligent/foolish, kind/cruel,* and *brave/cowardly.* (Students might also group synonyms, discussing the subtleties distinguishing the words.)

Students then discuss and support the paired adjectives by identifying the character's behavior that prompted each description. When I ask for a generalization about the character, I am apt to hear, "Luther has a complex personality" and "Luther is a dynamic character," as students realize that one character might possess conflicting traits or might undergo personality changes during the story.

I end the class by assigning a written character analysis. Students realize that most of the prewriting activities were done by the class as a whole. The adjective pairs and related discussion provide students with an ample supply of main points and supporting details for their papers, and they are able to describe their characters in precise terms. A class generalization might make a topic sentence. The prewriting activity makes the students' first attempt at character analysis relatively painless and provides them with a familiar procedure for future analysis.

Karin L. Weingart, Columbiana High School, Columbiana, Ohio

Trying Out a New Identity

Borrowing an idea from Harper Lee in *To Kill a Mockingbird,* that understanding comes from walking around in the other person's skin, I have devised an activity that helps students develop imaginative insight into character study. They are then more able to discuss various literary characters and poetic images.

Using the overhead projector, I display a poem entitled "Learn to Think Lizard" by Sue Moore. I found the poem in *Finding Your Life Mission* (ed. Naomi Stephan, Stillpoint Publishing, 1989). Moore encourages the reader to think like a lizard and "slink past the obvious to the underneath leaf."

Students read the poem line by line, stanza by stanza. They discuss the various images that they encounter and then focus on the theme of the poem. Students extend their imaginations and try to picture themselves as watercress or lizards. They might suggest other images of objects or animals and might write their own poems about learning to "think mountain goat" or "think lady's slipper," describing their new perception of the world around them.

Through this imaginative activity students will more easily understand the verbal portrait of the various characters they encounter in the works of fiction we read or, for that matter, in real life. Like the lizard, they will learn to go beyond what is apparent and reach "the underneath leaf," so that they can extend their understanding and appreciation of literary characters in subsequent writings and discussions. A typical direction to students after this lesson might be to "Think Hamlet" or "Think Jane Eyre."

Rose Gordy, Thomas S. Wootton High School, Rockville, Maryland

Modernizing Mythology

Trying to come up with ideas to interest high school students in mythology can be a challenge. Before I developed my modern mythology unit, I tried many ideas.

Some years students gave speeches as one of the mythological gods, goddesses, or heroes. The class then asked personal questions about their lives. Students had to do extensive research and internalize their character's personality and life. Additionally, they applied writing techniques to prepare a written copy of their speech and speaking techniques in delivering the speech. This worked well enough, but I wanted a better way to capture students' attention.

Other years students prepared projects—such as illustrated books on the constellations and their mythical connections, family albums of the gods, mobiles to accompany reports, illustrated dictionaries of words derived from myths, and posters illustrating their stories. The results were truly creative, but still not quite what I wanted.

One year the students formed groups, chose a myth, wrote a script, and presented the play to the class. Students learned a great deal from this activity and seemed to enjoy it, but still the myths seemed old-fashioned to them. I needed to make the stories more meaningful.

My solution was to have students once again write a play, but this time I asked them to modernize the story—to introduce contemporary characters, a contemporary setting, and contemporary language. This was the missing element. Students relished the assignment. In their modern versions, Phaëthon drove his father's powerful car, and Icarus piloted his father's plane. Medusa became a budding starlet who dared to compare herself to a movie queen, and Arachne boasted that she could weave better than the best Persian rug weaver.

Before students began their modernization, I needed to "set the stage." I explained at the outset of the unit that they would be writing a modern play based on one of the myths they read or heard, which gave them the chance to think about modernizing each story that they encountered. Next, I read some of my favorite myths aloud, we viewed filmstrips of other myths in class, and students read still more myths as homework or oral class reading. At this point I gave them the final guidelines for the assignment. The first year I presented my own modernized myth as a model. In subsequent years I used previous students' myths as examples. I read a few aloud and circulated others for students to read.

During the writing stage, students worked on their plays daily while I monitored their progress. I gave them a tentative due date and then announced the final deadline when most groups had nearly completed their scripts.

Writing modernized plays based on the classical myths has been much more successful with my students than writing the traditional plays. Everyone eagerly waited to hear and see the other groups' presentations or to read manuscripts from other classes. Not only did students' excitement and interest grow, but they readily acquired more expertise in writing techniques such as dialogue and writing elements such as characterization. More importantly, they made the connection between the ancient myths and life as it is lived today.

Janet Stroman, New Caney Middle School, New Caney, Texas

Collaborating to Learn

With my English literature class numbering close to thirty students, I use collaborative learning activities to activate those students who tend not to participate voluntarily in class discussions.

The following exercise has worked well when we study four medieval ballads: "Edward," "Sir Patrick Spence," "Get Up and Bar the Door," and "The Demon Lover." Students read all four ballads as a homework assignment and then divide into four groups. I often have them number off from one to four, with all the "ones" forming one group, all the "twos" forming a second group, and so on. The groups contain seven or eight students, so each group usually ends up with someone able to lead the discussion.

Each group is assigned one ballad and given the following instructions.

> You will have about 20 minutes to complete this activity, so you will have to stay on task and work quickly. First, decide who will do what. The choices are as follows.
>
> 1. One person reads the poem aloud to the group. Indicate in your journal that you are the reader.
> 2. In your group, discuss the story told in the ballad. One person should be prepared to *summarize the story* in the poem for the class. Put your summary in your journal.
> 3. In your group, discuss the tone of the ballad. One person should be prepared to discuss the *tone* of the poem with the class. Usually ballads are tragic. Is this one? How can you tell? Put your explanation in your journal.
> 4. In your group, discuss repetition in the ballad. One person should be prepared to explain *repetition* in your ballad to the class. What are the effects of repetition in this ballad? Put your explanation in your journal.
> 5. In your group, discuss the use of stanzas in the ballad. One person should be prepared to explain to the class how the *stanza structure* moves the story along. What is the subject of each stanza? What does each stanza contribute to the whole? Put your explanation in your journal.
> 6. In your group, discuss the questions on your ballad that appear in the textbook. One person should be prepared to discuss the *responses to these questions* with the class. Put your responses in your journal. (Person #8 will help with this.)
> 7. In your group, discuss how the ballad is relevant today. One person should be prepared to discuss your ballad's *relevance*

with the class. What ideas or lessons does it present that still apply today? Put your ideas in your journal.

While one person is responsible for each of the above tasks, I might call on anyone in the group to share his or her comments. Be sure that everyone understands each of these concepts.

Students are given only twenty minutes to complete the assignment, so they must stay on task. If strong discussions are going on at the end of this time period, I will extend the time five minutes. Since each student has a task and since everyone has to be familiar with all topics discussed, students tend to discuss the assigned ballad quite intensely.

Insights gained through the small-group discussions and notes written in their journals give students, including the quieter ones, confidence in sharing their ideas with the whole class. Through the group reports, everyone hears an explanation of all four ballads and others' insights about them. The assignment is truly a collaborative effort.

Jane A. Beem, Warren Township High School, Gurnee, Illinois

Stream-of-Consciousness Writing

Unless students are adequately prepared, reading works that employ the stream-of-consciousness technique may seem baffling to students. I use the following activity to prepare my students for reading "The Jilting of Granny Weatherall" by Katherine Anne Porter.

Several days in advance, locate a rock video that presents some sort of plot. I tape several hours from a video program and use the search feature on the VCR to find a video that is suitable for the classroom.

Show the video to the class and encourage them to discuss it. What story does it tell? How was the story presented? How was the video's plot presented differently from that of the usual movie or TV sitcom? Lead students to conclude that alternate methods of plot development are acceptable, and point out that the video's use of visual images still imparts a story line of sorts.

Ask students to close their eyes and to *think* for two minutes. Explain that no communication is acceptable and that they are not to doze off. Next, have them backtrack their thought progression: What were you just thinking of? What led you to that thought? What came before that?

Students are generally amused to see the variety and progression of thoughts they have entertained during their interior monologues.

Explain the connection: one alternate method of plot development involves telling the story through the thoughts of a major character. Point out that thoughts are often partial sentences without punctuation.

Once students have traced their own thought processes, they are ready to read Porter's story and are better able to follow the progression of Granny Weatherall's thoughts.

As a follow-up to reading and discussing the story, students may enjoy attempting to emulate the stream-of-consciousness technique. Here are some sample prompts, but students may have their own creative approaches:

1. You see "Mr. Right" or "Ms. Right" walking toward you in a crowded hallway.
2. The teacher walks toward your desk and places a test paper upside down on the desk. You reach to turn the paper over and see your grade.
3. The phone *finally* rings, and you extend your hand to answer it.
4. You hear a grinding of metal, lurch to a stop, and get out of the car to survey the damage.
5. You approach your home two hours after your curfew, knowing someone is waiting for you. You open the door to face the encounter.
6. You see the ball coming directly toward you and reach to catch it.

Students assume the persona of a character of their choice and record that character's thoughts during these brief moments, writing in the first person or third person.

Erma L. Richter, Port Neches-Groves High School, Port Neches, Texas

A Sound Approach to the Puritan Writers

Although I love teaching British literature, I have been less than successful with the Puritan writers. In the past my students have found Milton's elevated diction inaccessible and have failed to grasp the subtleties of *Pilgrim's Progress*. But last year that changed.

I introduced the writers of the Puritan period. My students read, had an open-book quiz on, and discussed the two Milton sonnets in our literature text. But before I introduced excerpts from *Paradise Lost*, I played the Rolling Stones' song "Sympathy for the Devil" without mentioning its title. For those not familiar with the song, it is not until the end that Lucifer reveals himself as the speaker. Then I asked students to talk about how the Stones had portrayed the devil. In our unit on Chaucer, we had studied the techniques an author has available to reveal a character, so students were able to speak convincingly about the time frame used (from Christ's time to the present) and the historical events the Stones had chosen to show Lucifer's evil nature (Christ's crucifixion, the killing of Czar Nicholas of Russia, the German blitzkrieg, the assassination of the Kennedys, and the harsh treatment of the Indians by the British when laying the railroad on the Indian subcontinent). Many students also mentioned that since Lucifer is telling his own story, he does not come across as negatively as he does in other literature they had read, although he is threatening by the end of the song.

At this point the class began *Paradise Lost,* paying particular attention to Milton's characterization of Satan. After hearing the Stones' song, students were more receptive to Milton's portrayal of Satan, and our study of this difficult piece went well.

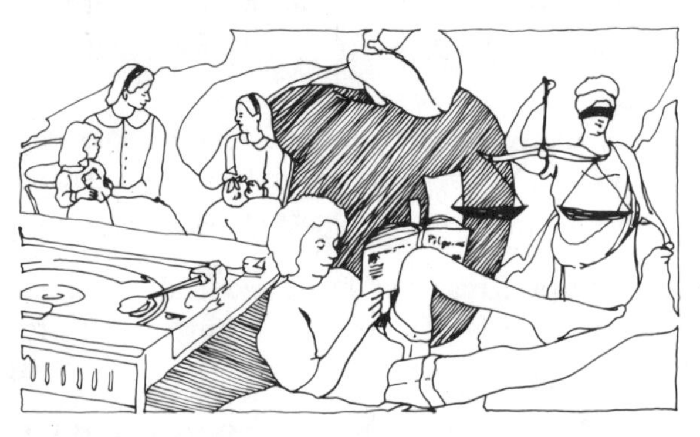

I tried the same technique with *Pilgrim's Progress.* I first played Tracy Chapman's "All That You Have Is Your Soul," in which a mother cautions her children not to be tempted by the "shiny apple" and to hunger instead for the taste of justice and truth. We spent time talking about the theme of this song and then moved on to Bunyan's work, focusing on its theme. Students were more receptive to Christian's plight, recognizing that all he had was his soul. Again the music had piqued their interest and drawn them into the literary work.

I also was aided in our discussion of Bunyan's work by the map in our textbook depicting the treacherous road the pilgrims traveled from the

City of Destruction to Heaven. This visual representation of the journey added still another element to our study of *Pilgrim's Progress*.

Our unit on Puritan writers concluded with a writing assignment on either pair of pieces—the Rolling Stones and John Milton, or Tracy Chapman and John Bunyan. I gave specific directions for students to include quotations in their papers since in previous assignments they had made general statements without supporting these ideas with specific citations. I was delighted to receive the best essays that I have read in ten years of teaching. I can honestly say that I look forward to the unit on Milton and Bunyan this year.

Serena Roberts-Bauer, Bellaire High School, Bellaire, Texas

Active Involvement with *Romeo and Juliet*

It is no secret that many students approach Shakespeare's works with hesitation and insecurity. For this reason I attempted to establish a new meeting ground between my ninth-grade students and Shakespeare's *Romeo and Juliet*.

I wanted to get my students excited about the unit, so I began by polling them about their hobbies and interests. Based on these findings, I decided to divide the class into five activity groups. I tried to accommodate students' first choices, but I also took into consideration who the leaders were and who worked well together.

Each group was assigned specific goals and responsibilities:

Artwork Group (artists)

1. To decide which scene in each act is the most important and to be able to explain its significance.
2. To capture the scene through some art medium. (My classes chose poster board.)

Plot Summary (writers)

1. To choose relevant events and construct a plot summary for each act.
2. To transfer their summary to the artwork group's poster. (They chose calligraphy pens.)
3. To explain the progressive movement of the plot from the introduction to the conclusion.

Characterization (actors and readers)

1. To develop character sketches of the most important characters in each act.
2. To note any character's developmental changes in personality throughout the play.

Analysis (good readers)

1. To search for and explain any significant literary devices used in each act.

Building (craftspeople)

1. To research and collect information about the Globe Theatre.
2. To build a replica of the Globe Theatre.

Every other day the class met as a whole. We would read an act aloud or listen to recorded excerpts, followed by a discussion of each act and an occasional quiz.

Following a day of reading came an activity day. On these days the two classroom coordinators (selected prior to the unit) sent the five groups off to different areas of the room as designated by signs. The groups, headed by a leader that I selected, spent approximately thirty minutes searching for information related to their particular topic. At the end of this time period, the class coordinators had the class reconvene to share the information that the groups had discovered. The new information was recorded on charts and review sheets that students kept in their Shakespeare notebooks. The building crew presented all its findings and the replica of the Globe Theatre at the completion of the unit.

My students and I have enjoyed this approach to *Romeo and Juliet* since everyone is involved in the teaching and learning process. Each student has an opportunity to collaborate with others and to share what he or she has discovered. Students also are allowed to use their talents and interests in order to accomplish group and individual goals. More importantly, students are given the chance to take on new responsibilities for their own learning and feel a sense of accomplishment in the classroom.

Kim Evans, Lamar 9th Grade Campus, Bryan, Texas

Dear Arthur Dimmesdale

Creative writing projects may provide an alternative to the usual expository writing assignments on symbolism and imagery in *The Scar-*

let Letter. While students may have difficulty deciphering Hawthorne's vocabulary and syntax, they can readily identify with a person betrayed by a loved one, with a child desperately wanting his or her family to be together, or with an individual at odds with society's rules and values.

We have devised a few activities that help make studying *The Scarlet Letter* a creative learning experience for students. They have an opportunity to analyze conflict, motive, and characterization. In addition, students develop creative writing skills as they incorporate dialogue and work within the genres of the dramatic monologue and the letter. Perhaps more importantly, these activities allow students the opportunity to empathize with the characters in the novel as they view life events from different perspectives.

In the first activity, students assume the role of Hester Prynne and write a long letter to Arthur Dimmesdale. They are given the following directions:

> Hester lets it all hang out! Frustrated at assuming the role of a single parent when she has both a husband and a lover, Hester writes a long letter to Arthur Dimmesdale. As Hester, describe your feelings about being alone in raising Pearl, about coping with Pearl's incessant questions about her origin, about dealing with threats to remove Pearl from your custody, about being alone and not being able to express your loving and passionate nature, and about realizing that Pearl is searching for a father and is being denied that experience.

In the second activity, students trace the development of a character throughout the novel by writing an imaginary dialogue between Pearl and her psychologist. Students receive these directions:

> This child needs help! Pretend that Pearl is airing her insecurities to a noted child psychologist. Pearl talks freely about the other Puritan children who ostracize her, about being brought up by her mother and without a father, about her uneasiness and curiosity about the scarlet letter, and about her feelings toward Dimmesdale and Chillingworth.

An excellent follow-up activity is the creation of a soap-opera script (we entitle ours "As the Letter Burns"). The class is divided into groups of four students each. Each group writes an original script—soap-opera style—of a scene, real or imagined, between Hester, Dimmesdale,

Chillingworth, and Pearl. Later, all groups act out their scripts, adding simple costumes, props, or music to make their scenes come alive. Our students have enjoyed the creative challenge and have presented some wonderful dramatic scenes, including a candlelight soliloquy by Dimmesdale as he explores his innermost guilt and turmoil and a scaffold scene featuring Hester singing a song of remorse at Dimmesdale's death.

The possibilities for creative scripts and the individual letter and dialogue are limited only by students' imaginations. The three activities are an enjoyable way to extend students' conceptions of the conflicts within *The Scarlet Letter.*

Elizabeth Smith and Gaile Emerson, Denton Senior High School, Denton, Texas

Personal Poem

As my college-prep American literature class neared completion of a four-week unit on Arthur Miller's *The Crucible,* I consulted numerous ideas that I had received from a summer writing course. What could my juniors do as a culminating activity? I eventually decided on an idea from CeCe Skala of Los Osos, California (who first heard it from Mimi Wheatwind of Albuquerque, New Mexico): using the "Personal Poem" with characters from a work of literature or history.

By this time students were well familiar with the drama. We had read Acts I and II aloud in class, with students alternating parts so that all had the opportunity to read. We listened to Acts III and IV on audiotape, which students seemed to like. Realizations like "Oh, so *that's* how I'm supposed to react!" or "Is that what the girls sounded like in the courtroom?" echoed throughout the classroom. We also read various short stories that had the same themes as *The Crucible:* "Young Goodman Brown" by Nathaniel Hawthorne, "The Lottery" by Shirley Jackson, and "A Piece of String" by Guy de Maupassant. Students gave a short speech on a particular character from the drama and wrote various journal entries, some of which were shared in class.

It was time for the Personal Poem assignment. I passed out the following format for students to follow as they wrote their poems:

Tell me your name.

What is your REAL name (not necessarily the name you go by, but a name you wish were yours, or a name you feel is true for you)?

Name the animal inside you. Explain your choice.

There's an object inside your heart. What is it? Explain its significance.

There's a word written on your forehead. What is it? Explain.

Tell me a sound you love. Tell me a sound you hate.

Tell me a smell you love. Tell me a smell you hate.

What is your favorite time of day? Why?

If your hands could speak, what would they say?

Tell me something you remember from your childhood.

Tell me a phrase or saying your mother/father/grandparents said to you often. (This may be in another language besides English.)

I then listed just seven characters on the board: Abigail Williams, John Proctor, Elizabeth Proctor, Reverend Parris, Tituba, Deputy Governor Danforth, and Reverend Hale. (Others, however, could be listed as well—perhaps Mary Warren and Giles Corey.) Students picked any character they wished, assumed that character's persona, and wrote a Personal Poem in response to the questions posed.

The results were fabulous! Students took the assignment seriously and described their new personas with insightful poems, exaggerated poems, and humorous poems. Some lines indicated students' own feelings about a character, but for the most part they were able to retain the character's persona. An example of a Personal Poem follows.

Elizabeth Proctor by Kelly N.

I am Elizabeth Proctor. I answer to Goody Proctor, Elizabeth, or mother.

The name I should answer to is "giving." I give my own freedom to save others.

A dove is what I am, pure, sweet, and watching over others. Pins are in my heart; I've been stuck by so many.

"Truth" is written on my forehead, for I've never lied, except once.

I love to smell my dinner cooking for my dear John, and I love to hear my children's laughter.

I am so tired of the stench in the jail, and I hate the chains that bound my hands together.

I love the morning when there is a fresh, new start to everything.

If my hands could speak, they would tell me to stop working so hard.

I remember my parents treating me with such kindness and respect. I remember my father telling me that I represent good.

I don't anymore.

Joanne M. Dillard, Morro Bay High School, Morro Bay, California

Teaching Thoreau

In our school, Thoreau's ideas always lead to wonderful class discussions. Both our American studies and American literature classes spend five to six hours on Thoreau, reading "Civil Disobedience" and excerpts from *Walden* and watching the film *Talking with Thoreau* or a video of "The Night Thoreau Spent in Jail," as performed in our school a few years ago. The following teaching approaches encourage students to experience Thoreau's ideas more directly. I have refined these activities over many years of teaching, but I do owe some credit to my colleagues Ron Gould and Diane Anderson.

"Civil Disobedience" : An Experiment in Action and Consequences

At some point in our discussion of "Civil Disobedience," I tell students to listen to me carefully, for I will give them some important directions and will answer no questions. My directions run like this: "Do something Thoreau would do. We will discuss what you did in twenty minutes." To the inevitable questions ("May we leave the room?" "Can we break school rules?"), I offer no answers.

Students in the past have used the twenty minutes to study an ant in the grass, go to the lily pond on our campus and watch the fish, and play on the swings near the junior school. They have called a local army base to protest military expenditures on the use of nuclear weapons; they have called the mayor's office or the governor's office to protest new construction of buildings or highways. On a more local level, they have broken school rules: eating in the library, changing into shorts, and taking a book out of the library without checking it out. And they have stayed in the room to use the time to study for a physics test. Someone always returns late to the discussion, breaking another rule.

In the discussion that follows, students describe how they used the time and explain why Thoreau might have done the same thing. They recognize their behavior as acts of civil disobedience.

At this point I remind students that good citizenship requires certain obligations and responsibilities. I explain that I am grading students on citizenship. All students will automatically receive an *A* unless they earn "demerits" by breaking school rules. In the course of the student presentations, whenever a student indicates a behavior that broke a rule (which could include leaving the classroom, since I had carefully not granted permission for that action), I write out a demerit slip. Invariably, some students become upset, but others recognize the connection to Thoreau; he did what he believed and accepted his "demerits"—his night in jail. The discussion tends to become pretty lively as students judge what consequences they are willing to face for specific actions and what "purer sources of truth" they might follow. By the time the class ends, students sometimes even question why I destroy the demerit slips—and some keep them as souvenirs.

Walden: An Experiment in Peace and Observation

We usually spend a class period outdoors while discussing *Walden,* finding a quiet, attractive location, closing our eyes, and experiencing what we can of nature in the midst of a city.

This year we tried a "trust walk," in which students pair up with another student. One student closes or blindfolds his or her eyes, and the second student introduces him or her to a newly perceived vision of our world. In the discussion that followed, students concluded that they noticed sensations that they might otherwise have overlooked. Both leaders and "sightless" students experienced a great deal. Comments included such remarks as "I never knew there were so many birds on campus"; "I could smell the dampness in the tree, and the bark scraped my nose"; "I felt the wind lift the hair on my arms."

Students rapidly make the connection to Thoreau (and to Emerson—one girl said she felt like "a transparent eyeball"). They realized that they spoke more softly and that the atmosphere in the group was calmer. Like Thoreau, they knew they "had several more lives to live," but as they left for their next class, they said that they felt ready to go back to civilization and felt a little less "desperate" in their "haste to succeed."

Follow-up Papers

I use a writing assignment to conclude our study of Thoreau. I have had particular success asking students to describe a meeting between Thoreau and another character or person from the course. Melville's Captain Vere, Hawthorne's Hester Prynne, Twain's Huck Finn, Martin Luther King, Jr., and Abraham Lincoln have all worked. The resulting papers have included dialogues, one-act plays, and extended poems; the settings have featured meetings in heaven, hell, and purgatory, on shipboard, and on a raft. The approach seems to spark the students' imaginations while allowing them to explore the ideas of important individuals or works of literature. The resulting papers are among the most successful student papers I read each year.

Susan R. Gorsky, Punahou School, Honolulu, Hawaii

Extending Meaning in Literature

I sent my literature students home with a half-sheet of paper and the assignment to retell Browning's "My Last Duchess." Despite the complaints of "I didn't get it at all" that greeted me at our next class, I collected all the papers and began reading them aloud to the class without revealing the writer. I refused to comment on whether each retelling was right or wrong.

When I completed the reading, students recognized some commonalities in the papers. What they did not realize was that the entire meaning of the poem was woven through the comments.

I had students form groups and handed out several of the "retell sheets" to each group. Students collaborated to piece together "My Last Duchess" from the common responses, thus bolstering their confidence in their ability to determine the meaning of poetry.

Next I asked students to extend the meaning of the poem into another genre. I suggested writing an obituary—if, in fact, the Duke did kill his wife. Students enthusiastically brainstormed other suggestions: a wedding announcement, a eulogy, a mystery story, another poem, a dialogue between a police officer and the Duke, a television newscast, a radio broadcast, a newspaper article, a bulletin regarding a missing person, a talk show discussion. Here is an obituary written by one student:

> Duchess, beloved wife of Duke. Born in 1594; died in 1614 at age 20. Member of White Mule Society, Sunset Watchers, and Smilers Unlimited, Inc. Died mysteriously while enroute on an extensive journey. The remains of the Duchess will not be publicly viewed out of respect for her grieving husband, the Duke. The family requests large, VERY LARGE, monetary memorials be sent to the Duke.

Once the extended writings were complete, students met in small groups once again and read their compositions aloud amid laughter and cries of "You gotta read this to the class!" They did, and we all laughed. I read mine aloud, too, because I write along with my students and share in their groups.

Humor, understanding, enthusiasm, and good writing all evolved from the poem that many students initially insisted they could not comprehend. This same approach would work with any piece of writing, poetry or not. Whenever students are given the chance to make sense out of literature, to break out of a conventional genre and select their own, and when they keep their audience and the situation in mind, then their best writing emerges.

Marybeth Tessmer, Pinconning Area Middle School, Pinconning, Michigan

3 Prewriting and Writing

Clear, effective writing by students is a goal we all strive to accomplish. We know that students learn to write by writing, and we try to provide a variety of writing experiences to help students develop into confident, accomplished writers. The ideas in this section are designed to encourage the flow of words and ideas and to stimulate students' interest in writing. Included are activities in which students write about art and write to music, a plan for establishing teacher-student correspondence, and strategies for producing descriptive writing, explanatory writing, composite autobiographies, and fictional research reports. Students start out their writing by "looping," evaluate their own progress in writing with journal self-assessments, reflect on completed essay assignments, and are honored at a writing assembly.

Getting Started with Looping

Looping, a prewriting activity designed to draw forth thoughts, memories, and responses to a subject, originated with Peter Elbow in his book *Writing without Teachers* (Oxford University Press, 1973). I have adapted the activity by adding the use of colored index cards for each stage of the loop. (The 3″ × 5″ size might be sufficient for reticent writers, but the roomier 4″ × 6″ size accommodates more writing.)

The index cards remove the "blank-page" syndrome that so many students experience and provide a tangible way to visualize the progression from each loop. It is important to remember that this is prewriting—no editing should take place. Students should write freely, letting their thoughts take them to undiscovered places.

Here are the instructions I give to students:

1. On a colored index card, write the topic you wish to explore on the top line, centered.

2. Write nonstop for 3–5 minutes. [I start with 2–3 minutes and progress students to longer periods of writing.] You may continue on the back of the card.
3. After reading what you have written, circle one of the following:
   a. a word or phrase you really like
   b. something you found interesting in what you wrote
   c. the phrase or sentence that captures what you want to say

This is Elbow's "center of gravity." Students then write that word, phrase, or sentence at the top of the next index card and follow the three steps. The process is repeated for a total of three cards. Each card is separate, yet it is linked back to the preceding card by the repeated word, phrase, or sentence.

Students then reread the three cards and determine what it is they want to say about a particular topic. This activity has been successful in helping students focus on creative writing assignments or in following research into a topic.

Terry A. Sansom, Round Rock Independent School District, Round Rock, Texas

Famous People Gallery

This first-day activity was suggested to me by Vergie M. McIntyre of Western Carolina University, Cullowhee, North Carolina. It helps put junior high and middle school students at ease and provides a nice introduction to a writing assignment.

I have the students form four groups and hand each group a large tagboard sheet on which I have glued pictures of famous actors, sports figures, entertainers, past presidents and other heads of state, or any celebrity figure that students will recognize. (*Time, Newsweek,* and *People* magazines are a good source of color photographs.)

Working in the groups, students identify the celebrities on their charts and make individual lists of names. Then we rotate the charts so that each group eventually sees each chart. I allow about ten minutes for students to list the names of all the celebrities they can identify. A contest might motivate students, with a small prize awarded to the winning group.

As a homework assignment, students are to select one person from their lists of names and to write a one-page essay explaining why this person is famous. Or they might deliver an oral presentation the following day. Younger students might enjoy trying to categorize the different celebrities.

Patricia W. Newman, Fairview Elementary School, Sylva, North Carolina

A Letter to My Students

This simple idea has become my favorite writing assignment for my students. At the end of every grading period (we have six where I teach), I write one letter that I copy for all my students. In my letter I tell them how I feel about their performance the past six weeks, give them a preview of what is ahead, and focus on any potential problems that we might have to deal with as a class. (Of course, I never single out individuals in my letters.) This is also a personal letter, and I usually relate some information about my family life, my endeavors as a writer, and such trivial things as music I've listened to lately, movies I've seen, and occasional commentary on current events.

The students' assignment, obviously, is to write me back. Their letters are the one writing assignment that I keep confidential (unless a situation warrants outside intervention). I encourage them to be honest about my class and to feel free to tell me anything they like. I have learned about everything from cheating rings to the latest infatuations to serious suicidal contemplation through these letters. Since the focus is on honest communication, students respond very positively to the assignment.

What I like best about this assignment is that it keeps me in touch with my students. The key to its success is for me to write a genuine letter to begin with. Then students feel free to make suggestions about improving a particular assignment, to comment on aspects of the class they dislike, or to reveal details from their personal lives.

Dallin Malmgren, Samuel Clemens High School, Schertz, Texas

Reflecting on Writing

One of the workshops I attended at the NCTE Convention in Baltimore in 1989 focused on encouraging students to evaluate and improve the process they used in producing a piece of writing. I decided to put this into practice upon my return.

My sophomores had written an essay on *Our Town* during my absence. I asked them to reread their essays and to answer as completely as possible the following questions:

1. What does the essay question mean to you?
2. Describe the steps you took as you went about answering the question (for example, made an outline, looked through notes and handouts, reread sections of the play in the textbook).
3. What problems did you encounter in your writing? (Was time a problem? Had you not paid careful enough attention to the play or to the class discussion?)
4. What does your title mean? How did you select it as the best possible title for your essay?
5. What did you do to avoid careless mistakes or mechanical errors? (Nothing? Proofread? Used a dictionary? Rewrote a rough draft?)
6. How do you feel about your finished product?
7. If you were to do this assignment over again, what would you do differently?
8. If you were assigning this essay a grade, what would it be and why?

Answering these questions encouraged students to reflect upon their writing. They thought about their content and methodology, and the questions offered some subtle suggestions about what they could have done. This gave students a logical starting place for revision. In addition, the responses helped me recap what had gone on in the classroom in my absence.

These questions would work equally well with essays on other literary works or with almost any other writing assignment.

Barbara A. Lutkenhaus, Somers High School, Lincolndale, New York

Journal Reviews for Self-Assessment

One of the hardest jobs a writing teacher has is to respond meaningfully to student journal entries. Naturally students want "credit" for their journal-writing efforts, but it is a long and sometimes tedious process for a teacher to read all entries and to make helpful, insightful comments to all students.

I prepare my students to evaluate their own progress in writing by doing self-assessments of their journals. Not only does this help alleviate some of the demands on my time, but, more importantly, students are thinking about their writing and their development as writers.

To accomplish the self-assessment, I ask students to review their journal entries, highlighting and recording all their commentary about writing—both positive and negative comments. If a passage is long, students can paraphrase rather than copy the entire passage.

Using a paper with headings like the following can help students organize their journal comments about writing:

Date Topic Journal Comments Attitude Change Indicated

After recording all their previous comments about writing, students should be able to see if there is any change or growth in their attitudes toward their writing. Invariably there will be, especially if the comments in the journal were recorded over a period of time. This is a perfect time for an essay about students' assessment of their own writing. That paper then becomes the major part of the evaluation process.

Norma Walrath Goldstein, Mississippi State University, Meridian, Mississippi

Sharing in a Writing Assembly

In the last few years the word *share* has become the word most often used in my senior composition classes. All writing assignments are shared in the classroom. I have seen great improvement in my students' writing, probably because students know their peers will see their work. But I believe the greatest benefit has been that the sharing of writing styles has caused students to experiment with different writing styles.

The most successful form of sharing that I use is our writing assembly. Three times a year my six classes receive the same writing assignment—for example, to write about a childhood memory. After the initial papers are completed, students might meet with a writing partner or in a small group to work on peer feedback and evaluation and then make revisions based on these suggestions. When the papers are in final form, each class is to select three papers to be read aloud at the assembly. Students might work in groups to read and discuss the essays, or they might read their own papers aloud to the whole class. Subsequent discussion emphasizes the merits of each essay and helps students identify which papers are the strongest.

These eighteen papers are read aloud by their authors at an in-school assembly for my six classes. We have printed programs and refreshments, and the eighteen authors are the guests of honor. Student judges select the top four papers, and these authors receive an award. Our student authors enjoy the attention given to their writing, and all the students are interested in what their classmates have written.

Donna J. Phillips, Springboro High School, Springboro, Ohio

The Art of Writing

This idea comes from a creative writing teachers course held at the Metropolitan Museum of New York in spring 1990. It is an effective way for students to increase their powers of observation through close examination of works of art and to encourage greater specificity and detail in their writing.

I start with a collection of color reproductions of paintings and ask each student to select a painting. They are to spend a few moments examining the painting and considering its effect on them. Then students are to prepare a brief written answer in response to the following questions:

> *Image:* Does the painting remind you of anything? an object? a person? a place?
>
> *Mood:* Is the image somber? angry? a feeling of gaiety?
>
> *Motion:* Is the painting active or static? Are you aware of brush strokes, gestures?
>
> *Sound:* Does the image give off a sound? Is it noisy? quiet?
>
> *Color:* Does one color predominate? Is it a varied palette?

After students have responded to their painting, they exchange paintings and respond to subsequent paintings. When everyone has commented on all the paintings, students make use of their initial responses as they complete one of the following writing assignments:

1. Write several lines of dialogue that might occur between people in the painting. Or write an interior monologue for a single person.
2. Write a passage describing the scene in the painting.
3. Use the five senses as a theme. What are the people in the painting hearing, smelling, touching, seeing, tasting?
4. Imagine that you are the artist who painted this picture. Write a letter to your brother or sister in which you describe the painting and how it came to be painted.
5. Choose one painting that has affected you more than the others and write about it. Use the words you previously recorded about that particular painting.

One student wrote the following description of Van Gogh's "Undergrowth with Two Figures." The underlined words are from his initial response sheet.

> The dark and dreary mood contrasts with the colorful flowers. The people look like dead statue-like ghosts just standing there, while the flowers blow briskly in the wind. The flowers look as if they are in a hollow tube, and there is movement of flowers hitting one another.
>
> The dark and gloomy still colors of the forest contrast with the bright, fragrant, and constantly moving flowers. This scene reminds me of my cross-country trips to national parks and looking at deer standing motionless, looking back at you with no other distractions or noise.
>
> Peter

Joseph A. Critelli, W. C. Mepham High School, Bellmore, New York

The Writing Process to Music

I bring classical music into the classroom as a stimulus to creative writing. This assignment has worked with students of all ability levels from grades 6 to 12.

I begin the activity with a discussion of how both written and musical compositions can tell a story or can express emotions or feelings. We talk about the parallelism between changes in the mood of music and paragraph changes in writing. Then I explain that I am going to play a piece of music two or three times. Students are to write a story about what they believe is happening in the music or to describe what they visualize when listening to the music. I find that giving them latitude in the assignment removes some of the fears of the more insecure or less creative writers.

I use Tchaikovsky's *1812 Overture* for this activity because it is a bold, dramatic work containing many changes in tone. Many other classical pieces would work as effectively. Some students have previously heard this symphony, but rarely does a student remember its historical significance. I do not reveal the title or background of the piece to students until the assignment is complete.

Then I turn on the music. Depending on the length of class and how much time we spend on the preliminary discussion, I may not play the entire symphony. As I play the work the first time, I ask students to brainstorm by jotting down any and every idea that comes to mind. I walk around the room to be sure that students are actually doing this. I find that some students just listen and want to wait on writing until the second playing, while others begin writing in paragraph form, skipping the brainstorming and organizational stages.

I play the music a second time, asking students to narrow their ideas and to organize them to the pattern of the music. Next comes the actual writing. Whether we listen to the music a third time is up to the class to decide. Some students want or need to hear the music once again to be sure that their writing fits the music; others find it distracting while they are writing.

When the writing is complete, students might edit their papers in class or as a homework assignment. Or they might work with a partner for peer editing and to compare their different responses to the music.

I always enjoy the creative ideas that students develop as they listen to the music. While I initially hear some complaints about listening to classical music, they usually enjoy this activity. Their stories often involve adventures on an epic scale, vivid descriptions of an important event in a student's life, or detailed visualizations of nature.

Evangeline A. Plaza, Concord, Tennessee

The Ups and Downs of Writing

Adrenalin pumping, pulse pounding, you watch with dread the approaching apex, trying not to think about the abyss on the other side. Then in rapid succession come the fall, the scream, the relief as the roller coaster slows, drifts, then crawls to a stop.

Such heady emotions can stimulate students to "experience" narration of events in reading and writing and can help them use the structure of the short story as a tool for improving their own narratives.

I begin by playing a sound track of a roller coaster ride, asking students to guess what they are hearing. (Most public libraries and many school libraries have sound track records. One source is *101 Sound Effects*, Gateway Records, New York, 1982.)

Listening a second time, we describe from our own experiences either roller coasters we have ridden or ones we have seen in movies. What did the car look like? Where and when was this ride? (Setting) How did we feel that day before the ride began? (Mood) We also consider the people who rode on the roller coaster—ourselves, our friends, and the blurry impression of other riders. (Characters)

The ride evoked a multitude of emotions. How did we feel as the car started forward and began to ascend? (Conflict) During the ride, the car changed directions or traveled up and down. (Rising action) However, near the end of the ride, the most exciting moment approached. What emotions accompanied reaching the arc and teetering at the highest point, finally glimpsing the descent to come? (Climax)

We talk about the inevitability of that rapid fall (Falling action) and the relief of slowing down and stopping. (Resolution) Although the scene at the end of the ride is similar to the one at the beginning, the characters have often been changed by the experience.

I then draw a diagram of a roller coaster ride on the board, labeling the points where they correspond to the plot line of a conventional short story. We examine a story like "Goldilocks and the Three Bears" and identify the points of its plot line. Then students form small groups and tell brief stories, discovering that everyone can tell a story.

Later the plot line is used to guide class discussions of selections from the literature text. While designed for the conventional story, the concept can be extended to include cliff-hangers and other plot variations or to clarify elements of character development (static or dynamic characters, major or minor characters).

At this point students are ready to experiment with story writing. After completing their narratives, students use a diagram of the roller coaster ride as a self-evaluation tool. They identify story elements in their own writing and label their diagrams as they locate the points. The drawing is useful during teacher-student conferences about their narratives.

The best aspect of this technique is that students discover that writing, like the roller coaster ride, has its problems and its ups and downs, but the end result is a thrilling experience.

Joan Berry, Canyon Vista Middle School, Austin, Texas

Not Just Another Autobiography

I was less than thrilled to spot *autobiography* on the curriculum specifications for the eleventh-grade literature course I was assigned to teach. Having to read thirty papers with the same "I was born/I went to school" format was not a pleasant thought. As I projected myself into my students' minds, I concluded that their reactions to the assignment would be as ho-hum as mine. So I decided to try a different approach.

I broke down the autobiography assignment into a series of smaller compositions written during the first six weeks of the course. Some of the following assignments were prepared in class, while others were homework assignments.

1. Use pictures, words, and phrases cut from magazines or newspapers to make a collage that represents your personality and interests. Write a one-page paper explaining the various elements in your collage.
2. Imagine that the year is 2001. What career or job will you have then? Be sure to include information about your interests, talents, and abilities that will lead to your success in this career.

3. Write a paper describing your dream house. Give specific details about the setting, exterior features, layout, and decor. What do you like best about your dream house?
4. Think about an incident from your past that taught you a lesson. It might involve you directly or a family member. Tell what happened and what you learned from the incident.
5. Draw a map on which you label all of the places where you have lived. This might be a city map, a state map, a regional map, a U.S. map, or even a world map, depending on just where you have lived previously. Write a composition in which you explain when and for how long you lived in each home. Describe one thing that you will always remember about each place of residence—your room, your home, your school, an event, a neighbor, a favorite place, something that made a vivid impression on you. If you have always lived in the same house or apartment, you might prepare a city map and describe favorite places in your community. Or your map and paper might focus on trips that you have taken.
6. Write a paper explaining how you got your first and middle names. Who named you? Are you named after someone? Does your name have any special meaning? Do you have a nickname? If so, what is the story behind it?
7. Imagine that you are to meet someone for the first time, perhaps at a crowded airport. Write a description of yourself so that you can be easily identified.

This writing was not done in isolation. I integrated the assignments with our literature selections. For example, after we read Abigail Adams's letter from the White House, students wrote about their dream house. The narrative about an incident that taught a lesson followed the reading of excerpts from Ben Franklin's autobiography.

Students spent three class periods in our computer lab using a word-processing program to type their compositions. They used the program Print Shop to design and print covers. Back in class, students assembled all of the autobiography components into a booklet: compositions, map, collage, and personalized cover. The completed autobiographies were then displayed around the room for everyone to enjoy.

My middle-level students enjoyed this approach to autobiographies far more than in the past, and I did too. Both the quality and the quantity of their writing increased, indicating they were improving their writing skills.

Sandra B. Pardue, Charles Lincoln Harper High School, Atlanta, Georgia

Fantasy Objects

To prepare my middle school students for a fantasy writing assignment and to encourage creativity, I hand out to each student a small plastic bag containing five toothpicks, two rubber bands, two paper clips, and a 6″ × 6″ piece of cardboard. I also have scissors, tape, and glue available.

Students have the next twenty-five minutes to create a fantasy object using as many of the items in the bag as possible. There are no restrictions on their designs; they are free to create any object they wish—a tool, an animal, a gadget, a piece of jewelry, a toy, a weapon, a decorative item, whatever.

Once the fantasy objects are complete, students select one of the following writing assignments:

1. Students assume the role of advertising manager for the company producing their fantasy object. They are to write the script for a television commercial advertising their product or the text for a magazine or newspaper ad. They should describe the use of their product and convince viewers/readers to buy the product.
2. Students write a children's story in which their creation plays a major role. The fantasy object might come to life and be the main character in the story, or it might retain its inanimate properties and serve as an important prop.
3. Students write a poem about this fantasy object. They can use any poetic format they wish as they describe the object, indicate their feelings for it, personify it, or ridicule it.

The writing assignments can be read aloud and then displayed in the classroom next to the particular fantasy object.

Hildegard Fuchs, Lincoln West High School, Cleveland, Ohio

Descriptive Writing

Credit for the following idea goes to my student teacher, Cynthia Tisdale, a graduate student at Furman University. She used the exercise to raise students' awareness to Faulkner's evocative descriptions in *Absalom, Absalom!* The lesson worked so well and generated such superb descriptive writing that I have expanded it.

Students begin with a homework assignment: write a paragraph of technical description that is roughly three-quarters of a page in length. The descriptions may be of any place they wish and should be photographic in clarity and detail, but they are to avoid any emotional tone in their writing.

The next day we discuss the differences between technical descriptions and emotive descriptions. Examples of both can be selected from current literature that the class is studying, or I might write simple paragraphs demonstrating the two types of description.

Students then work with one or two other students to write an emotive description of their classroom. After first drafts are completed, one student from each group reads the description aloud to the class. Generally a wide divergence of emotions will be presented—my students' descriptions of the classroom have ranged from a playroom to a torture chamber.

I then ask students to rewrite their technical descriptions twice—once to provoke a positive emotional response from the reader and once to provoke a negative emotional response. As they compare the two, they will recognize the power of descriptive writing to evoke emotions, which will help them be better writers and be more perceptive readers.

An extension of the lesson would be to rewrite the paragraph using no adjectives, only strong, specific verbs and clear, concrete nouns. This is especially appropriate when the class is studying a Hemingway novel.

Charles E. Templeton, Travelers Rest High School, Travelers Rest, South Carolina

A Fictional Research Paper

In my British literature class, I use an idea adapted from "Research Revisited; Or, How I Learned to Love the *Reader's Guide*" by Joseph

Peacock in the November 1987 *English Journal* (vol. 76, no. 7, pp. 57–60). The assignment works best second semester, after we have covered three or four periods of British literature.

Students are to put themselves in the role of a historical "novelist" and to write a research paper about a famous figure in British history. I hand out a list of possible topics suggested by myself and by previous and current students. It is an ongoing list to which we continually add and is intended to suggest possibilities rather than to restrict students. They are free to select their own research topics, with approval from me.

The research paper is organized into five chapters, several pictorial appendixes, and a bibliography. Students sometimes add prologues and epilogues. The paper is a narration; most students choose to write in first person, while some prefer third. The narrator may be the famous person, but more often it is a secretary, assistant, nurse, lady-in-waiting, groom, or some other fictional servant in the household of the famous person. Once the topic and main character are chosen (such as a nanny to Queen Victoria's children; a squire to Henry Howard, Earl of Surrey; a Southwark innkeeper in competition with Harry Bailey), the student scans available sources and considers how to organize the five chapters. I meet with each student, and together we select the subject for each chapter in order to focus on a particular sequence of events within a given time period.

Here is a sample of the type of ideas and sources a student might start with:

> An Emissary from Henry VIII to Pope Clement in Rome
>
> Biographical Details:
> only son of a court doctor and a lady-in-waiting
> born at Greenwich Palace in 1498
> former secretary to Cardinal Wolsey
> carried the first letters from England to the Vatican requesting the annulment of Henry's marriage
> married to the daughter of a court musician
> ordered from the court after execution of Anne Boleyn
> died impoverished in 1551
>
> Suggested Sources:
>
> | | |
> |---|---|
> | Henry VIII | Pope Clement |
> | Greenwich Palace | Catherine of Aragon |
> | Anne Boleyn | Cardinal Wolsey |

Suggested Appendixes:
map showing travels from England to Rome
Greenwich Palace
Henry, Catherine, Anne

The finished paper, "Henry's First Queen," contained the following table of contents. (Sir Edward Walker is Henry's emissary.)

Research Information Included:

Hampton Court Palace	Nonsuch Palace
Henry VIII	Catherine of Aragon
King Arthur	Anne Boleyn
Cardinal Wolsey	Duke of Richmond
Pope Clement	Holy Roman Emperor
Oliver Cromwell	Protestant Reformation
Thomas Cranmer	Church of England

It is important to select topics on which information is available. I made the mistake of suggesting a monk at Jarrow during the time of Bede and a faithful parish priest in London during the time of the plague, but books on church history do not abound in my small town. Every year students devise their own topics, and we add them to the list for future research papers. This year someone expressed interest in the Hundred Years' War and Joan of Arc, a topic that may be selected by a future student.

Especially popular topics have included a Viking invader during the time of Alfred the Great; knights in various crusades; an apprentice actor in Shakespeare's company; a member of the Gunpowder Plot; a neighbor of Samuel Pepys during the fire; a servant in the household of any of Henry's queens; a Norman soldier with William the Conqueror; a young priest with Thomas à Becket; and a pagan Celt living near Stonehenge.

While I know that historical fiction does not require documentation, I have students use internal documentation to help instill a knowledge of proper research paper form. They are to use a minimum of five sources, only one of which can be an encyclopedia.

As with any research paper, there is always some resistance to this assignment. However, I have never observed students as interested in their own papers or those of their fellow classmates. We put all the papers on display so everyone can enjoy them.

Karen L. Rieffel, Okeechobee High School, Okeechobee, Florida

Your Own Backyard

Students' awareness of their surroundings can be heightened as they examine a variety of lifestyles present within our country and discover the reasons for these differing lifestyles. The activity requires the participation of one or more teachers in other parts of the country. A point-and-shoot camera and a cassette tape player would be useful.

Begin by asking students what they know about lifestyles in various regions of the country. How much of this is based on personal experience? How much is based on conjecture? List these "facts" on the board and have a student scribe record the information. Then discuss some of the misinformation that people have about other parts of the country. For example, Denver is not in the middle of the mountains, and vegetable gardens do grow in Alaska.

Ask students to think about their own region of the country, their own backyard. What would they like people in other regions to know about their school and their community? What are some of the fun things to do? What are some things that a person should know before coming to live in the community? How could a person prepare in advance to feel less like a stranger? Students might brainstorm these ideas as a class activity or in small groups.

Once students have compiled a list of information about their community, they form small groups, with each group receiving a portion of the list to work on. (If the list is modest in length, each group might receive the entire list.) Students then brainstorm additional details and select the best ideas to include in a written report. Peer editing takes place naturally as students work together on the report.

Student artwork or photographs taken with a simple camera can show scenes of school life or highlight points of interest in the community, making the report look much like a travel brochure. Students whose report discusses the dialect of the area can include a tape recording of local speech patterns.

Once the reports are completed, the members of each group present their reports aloud, and class discussion follows. Copies of the reports are sent to the other schools that have agreed to take part in the project. When our class receives the reports prepared by the cooperating classes, students read about and discuss what life is like in another community. Comparisons are quickly made, and students try to identify reasons for the differing lifestyles.

This same activity would lend itself to an exchange agreement with a class in another country. Students would need to consider their particular audience when planning and writing their reports, perhaps providing more detail or explanation of customs that would be unfamiliar to a foreign audience. Or they might choose to be more general in their information so that more topics could be explored.

Joan K. Wilson, Everitt Junior High School, Wheat Ridge, Colorado

Cartoon Character Stories

Here's an idea that I adapted from visiting writer Jean Rukkile for writing short stories based on cartoon characters and situations. The activity works well in a short story unit or as a change-of-pace assignment at any time. The length of time devoted to the activity can range from one class period to as much as several days, depending on your purpose and how elaborate you would like the finished books to be. My students do quick first-draft writing, but this could be a more polished assignment.

Bring in a supply of cartoons with the captions cut off. Look for cartoons that involve character interaction. There should be enough cartoons for each student to receive four. My favorite cartoons are those found in *The New Yorker.* I find them a sheer delight and a good stimulus to writing, but cartoons from a newspaper or from other magazines would also work. Students might be asked to bring in cartoons as well, since the activity requires numerous cartoons.

Students will also need blank books that consist of a construction paper cover with four pages of white paper stapled inside. I use 8½″ × 11″ construction paper folded in half, but a larger size book might be needed if the cartoons are large. Students can easily make the booklets themselves, or they can be assembled beforehand.

I start by randomly distributing four cartoons to each student. Students select one cartoon and glue it to the first page inside their books. Using the cartoon to suggest a setting and characters, students write the opening to a short story. Allow only a short period of time (about five minutes) for this writing. You may vary this, but limiting the time forces students to think and write quickly.

Next, students glue a second cartoon on the second page and continue their same story, introducing new characters and settings as needed. They do the same with the remaining two cartoons, again continuing the same story. Students might wish to trade one cartoon with a nearby student if they feel one of their cartoons does not fit with the others.

Once students have incorporated all four cartoons into their stories, they may need additional time to complete some segments or to create transitions between segments. Allow them time to title the stories and to make any changes or corrections they wish, depending on how much time you wish to devote to revising. Then students can trade books and enjoy one another's cartoon character stories.

Shirley Kasper, Apache Junction High School, Apache Junction, Arizona

The Importance of Being Accurate

Explanatory, how-to writing ranges from the complex formal instructional manual to a simple note on how to get to someone's house. Yet despite its prevalence, how-to writing remains one of the most difficult to teach effectively to high school and college students.

Students may encounter several common problems in writing how-to essays. Certain key steps in the process may be omitted by oversight. The different parts of a product to be assembled may not be described well enough to distinguish easily between them. The order of the tasks to be completed may be unclear or jumbled. Not anticipating mistakes, defects, or changes sometimes results in confusion and frustration.

How, then, can we teach effective how-to writing to our students? My approach is not simply to tell students about the common problems that may plague their essays. Instead, I show them firsthand how their how-to descriptions affect real audiences who have a task to complete.

I start the activity by distributing to each student a set of six different colored gumdrops and seven toothpicks. Students pair off, and then the partners sit back to back with a hard, flat working surface before each of them, such as a desk or book. Designate one student in each pair as the instruction "giver" and the other as the instruction "receiver."

Each instruction giver individually constructs a unique three-dimensional figure using all the gumdrops and toothpicks. The figure is to rest on the desk or book, and at least one gumdrop must be raised above the surface. Next, the instruction giver communicates to the instruction receiver oral directions for building an identical three-dimensional figure.

During construction the giver cannot look to see if the receiver is implementing the instructions correctly and cannot ask if the receiver understands a command or has finished a task. The receiver cannot look at the giver's figure and cannot speak at all—he or she cannot ask for a command to be repeated or reworded and cannot ask for confirmation.

When all the gumdrop sculptures are completed, students may walk around and observe the varying degrees of accuracy attained by the other pairs. Then, as students dismantle their designs and eat the gumdrops, we talk about their experiences with receiving inadequate instructions and discuss the subsequent results—their anger, confusion, or frustration when they could not understand the directions and when their gumdrop figures did not match those created by their partners.

The gumdrop activity illustrates that how-to directions must be intricately detailed in order to be successful. When I give a how-to writing assignment for the following class period, students are more attuned to the importance of preparing accurate instructions.

Bruce McComiskey, Purdue University, West Lafayette, Indiana